Ankylosaurus

By Joanne Mattern
Illustrations by Jeffrey Mangiat

Reading Consultant: Susan Nations, M.Ed.,
author/literacy coach/consultant in literacy development
Science Consultant: Darla Zelenitsky, Ph. D.,
Assistant Professor of Dinosaur Paleontology at the University of Calgary, Canada

WEEKLY READER®
PUBLISHING

Please visit our web site at www.garethstevens.com.
For a free color catalog describing our list of high-quality books,
call 1-800-542-2595 (USA) or 1-800-387-3178 (Canada).
Our fax: 1-877-542-2596

Library of Congress Cataloging-in-Publication Data

Mattern, Joanne, 1963–
    Ankylosaurus / by Joanne Mattern ; illustrations by Jeffrey Mangiat.
      p. cm. — (Let's read about dinosaurs)
    Includes bibliographical references and index.
    ISBN-10: 0-8368-9415-4   ISBN-13: 978-0-8368-9415-8 (lib. bdg.)
    ISBN-10: 0-8368-9419-7   ISBN-13: 978-0-8368-9419-6 (softcover)
    1. Ankylosaurus—Juvenile literature. I. Mangiat, Jeffrey, ill. II. Title.
QE862.O65M248   2009
567.915—dc22   2008024771

This edition first published in 2009 by
Weekly Reader® Books
An Imprint of Gareth Stevens Publishing
1 Reader's Digest Road
Pleasantville, NY 10570-7000 USA

Executive Managing Editor: Lisa M. Herrington
Creative Director: Lisa Donovan
Senior Editor: Barbara Bakowski
Art Director: Ken Crossland
Publisher: Keith Garton

Printed in the United States of America

1 2 3 4 5 6 7 8 9 10 09 08

Table of Contents

Boldface words appear in the glossary.

Armed for Safety

Meet Ankylosaurus
(ang-kie-luh-SAWR-us).
This dinosaur was built
like a tank!

Ankylosaurus was covered with thick, heavy **plates**. Its skin was tough. This **armor**, or body covering, kept Ankylosaurus safe.

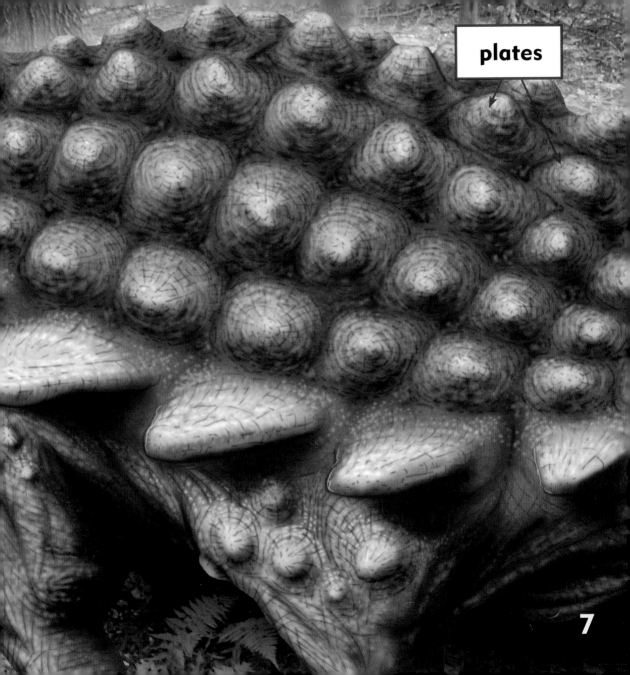

plates

This dinosaur had rows of **spikes** on its body. It had horns on its head.

spikes

Ankylosaurus had one more weapon. Its tail had a bony club at the end. Ankylosaurus could swing its tail to hurt attackers.

tail

bony club

11

Slow-Moving Giant

Ankylosaurus needed to protect itself. It had short legs and could not run fast.

13

The bones of this dinosaur were very thick. Even its **skull** was thick and heavy. It had a small brain inside that bony head!

ANKYLOSAURUS SKULL

15

Ankylosaurus was almost as long as two garbage trucks. This dinosaur weighed as much as two cars.

Plant Eater
of the Past

Ankylosaurus ate low plants.
Animals that eat plants
are called **herbivores**
(HER-buh-vorz).

Scientists have found Ankylosaurus **fossils** in western North America. Fossils tell a lot about the dinosaurs of long ago.

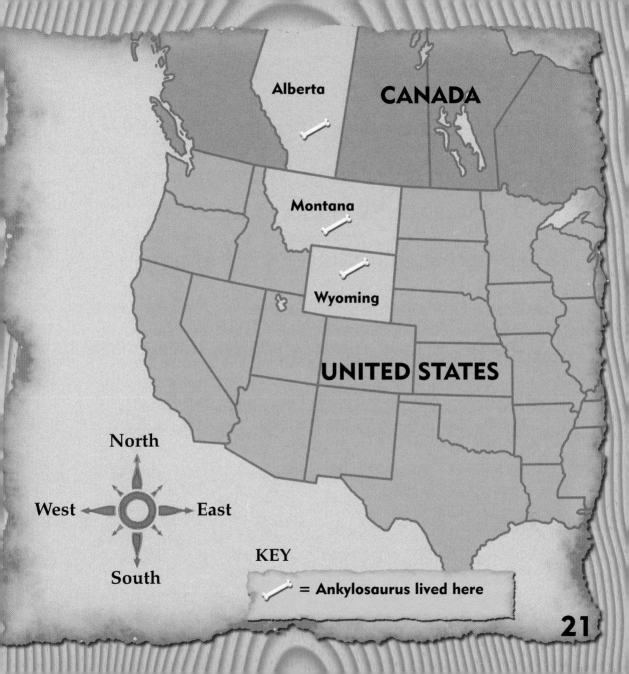

Alberta

CANADA

Montana

Wyoming

UNITED STATES

North

West ◄———●———► East

South

KEY

= Ankylosaurus lived here

Glossary

armor: a body covering for defense

fossils: bones or remains of animals and plants that lived long ago

herbivores: animals that eat plants

plates: flat pieces of bone

skull: the bones of the head

spikes: large, pointed pieces of bone that stick out

For More Information

Books

Ankylosaurus and Other Mountain Dinosaurs. Dougal Dixon (Picture Window Books, 2005)

I Am an Ankylosaurus. Karen Wallace (Atheneum, 2005)

Web Sites

Planet Dinosaur: Ankylosaurus
www.planetdinosaur.com/dinosaurs_a2z/A/ankylosaurus.htm
This site is filled with interesting information about Ankylosaurus.

Zoom Dinosaurs: Ankylosaurus
www.enchantedlearning.com/subjects/dinosaurs/dinos/Ankylosaurus
Find facts, pictures, maps, and printouts of Ankylosaurus.

Index

About the Author

Joanne Mattern has written more than 250 books for children. She has written about weird animals, sports, world cities, dinosaurs, and many other subjects. Joanne also works in her local library. She lives in New York state with her husband, four children, and assorted pets. She enjoys animals, music, reading, hiking, and visiting schools to talk about her books.